BEING ME IS ENOUGH... LGBTQ+

Lisa V. Taitt-Stevenson
Imani Andaye' Walker

DEDICATION

To the LGBTQ+ community which needs to be reminded that being themselves is more than enough; You are incredible as you are. We all need and want words of encouragement to enable us to take everything that this world throws at us; while balancing our lives, thoughts and opinions along with juggling what others may think is wrong or right about us. Know that as you are, and identify is more than enough. You do not need to change yourself in order to "fit in". While on this journey, consider the power of we, consider none of this needs to be done alone. Know that while on your journey, there are those that will walk it with you, cheer alongside you and carry you when needed. Rest, lean and allow the support to take you from one level to the next.

To all the lives lost, you are loved and you will never be forgotten.

Allow this book to be a reminder that in order for you to be considered enough, all you have to do is be your authentic self.

Accept it and walk boldly in it.

ACKNOWLEDGMENTS

From Lisa: To my mom who constantly supports me and sees things in me that I still don't see. You cheer louder than everyone else for me. Thanks for always being my rock.

From Imani: To the people that have surrounded me with love and support, and to my mother for allowing me to be me in all of my rainbow glory, and loving me through all things. Though this is my journey, there have been people in my life that ensured I didn't have to walk it alone. Whether the trip was a happy one or an emotional one, they remained. Thank you to all those that love me, and support my choice to be me.

BEING ME IS ENOUGH...
LGBTQ+

1

In all the hurt, Holding Onto Positive Energy will pull you through.

2

As I stand, regardless of how it looks, I will remember that I am never standing alone.

3

Today's Goal:

Look in the mirror…now smile. Feel better? You should. The person in the reflection does.

4

When there are
times I feel like
giving up, I will
remember all the
times I didn't...
so why start now.
Every time I
refuse to give up
I take a little
bit of my power
back.

5

In a perfect world help
is automatically given.
In this world, it isn't.
When in need, make it
known. Shout it from
the rooftops if you
aren't being heard.
There is no shame in
asking for help. We all
need help.

6

I am more than enough.

7

Love comes with no rules, no limitations and no hindrances. Love is inevitable, unavoidable, and unexpected. Love comes whether you want it or not. Love needs no invitation. Love is free. Love is rightfully yours. Love is not owned by any one person, it is the birthright of all people.

8

The next time you go looking for a pot of gold at the end of a rainbow, consider YOU ARE the treasure that you have been looking for.

9

I'm not sure why anyone would ostracize anyone else, last I checked we were all humans not ostriches.

10

I am strong. I draw strength from a place that only I can understand as it is mine. When you come into my life, you are more than welcome to fuel that strength, but if you are here to diminish it, then I must ask you to move on.

11

I realize that in order to make a change, my voice can't just be an echo to the complaint, but a contribution to the solution.

12

The character, in which I stand, is what should matter the most.

13

My desire for acceptance is not contingent upon someone else's rejection. As much as I may want their acceptance, I must first project acceptance for myself.

14

What I love, how
I love, and who
I love, does not
define the
quality of my
love.

15

Showing my emotions does not make me weak. There is strength in my ability to love beyond myself. There is power in my ability to shed tears for the community in which I live and love. There is courage in my ability to forgive my enemies, and there is valor in my ability to unconditionally love myself. Showing my emotions does not make me weak; showing my emotions makes me human.

16

luckily for me and those around me, how I live and how I love is not always determined by how I am "loved" or how one deems I should live.

17

Guess What?
You are closer
today than you
were yesterday.

18

When faced with hate, realize it's not so much about who you love, but another person's inability to comprehend unconditional love.

19

Wherever this life of love takes me, I will always remember to be present in the journey.

20

Today's Goal:

Take the time to look beyond the façade that someone else may be showing you. You never know what others are going through at any given moment.

21

Another day of life allows for another day of self-discovery.

22

Have *PRIDE* in your version of you, it's the only one that matters.

23

How I feel will never be a crime.

The only crime would be not feeling at all.

24

The only one
that has to be
comfortable
with me and
mine, is mine
and me.

25

I will not allow fear to hold me captive. In my world, fear will not paralyze me, but propel me. It will not hinder me but motivate me. Rather than allow fear to control me, I will control my fear.

26

Yes, you are loved. Do you hear me??? You are loved. Whether you feel it or not, it is there. This book represents love... love for you. Now do you feel it?

27

Everyone has the right to choose to be themselves or someone else. The problem with being someone else is the role is already taken. Do you want to be an understudy or the lead in your own production?

28

As I stand so will others.

Take a moment to realize when you stand, you are not standing as one, you are standing as many.

29

Today's goal:

Choose
happiness.

30

I will never forget
the power of "we".

31

Today's Goal:
Choose yourself.

32

Self-love is the blueprint on how you give love, receive love and recognize love.

33

I am worthy and deserving of life, support, love, encouragement, motivation, and security.

34

Every minute of every day is another opportunity for me to change things.

35

I am beautiful
inside and out.

36

Today's Goal:

1. Think happy thoughts:

2. Create your happy space:

3. Sing a happy song:

4. Do a happy dance:

5. Take a happy nap. (repeat daily)

37

I am not less than anything because anything less than would be downright unsavory.

38

I am filled with greatness. There are those that will question my abilities, my position, and my reason for being. Regardless of the questions and doubts, my greatness will never lose value.

39

Life wouldn't be easier without me... life would be empty without me.

40

I am here to win; win at life and win at love. I will know when I have won, because my win is defined by me.

41

To live a lie is saying that I am not worthy of the truth. Living a lie is exhausting; standing in truth is necessary.

42

As I walk along this journey called my life, I will stop to smell the roses, walk slow enough to take in its beauty, and run if I see a bee.

43

Rejection is the universe's way of telling you they aren't ready for you yet.

44

I am worth the starting of today and the starting of right now; There is no reason to delay me living my best life.

45

All that I have
endured and
weathered doesn't
have to change who I
am, unless I want it
to; The choice is mine.
I can choose to allow
it to make be bitter or
make me better.

46

I am more than
what the world's
perception of
"ME" is.

I am

More than Enough

47

I am not a broken item that needs to be "fixed".

48

I am not afraid of the commitment I make to myself. The commitment to truly be me; The commitment to the only me I will ever be.

49

I was not created to "fit" in a box, I was created to live as if there is no box.

50

I am not defined by any title given to me; I am defined by my character and if I don't like it, I have the ability to change it.

51

There is a beauty within me that the world hasn't even seen yet.

52

I am open to the kind of love that will uplift me, and fill me with the desire to be better and do better. The kind of love that will love me to the point that I begin to love myself.

53

I am a leader, a dreamer and an achiever. In all of these things I will be humble, fearless and tenacious. A humble leader, a fearless dreamer and a tenacious achiever.

54

The most beautiful rainbows form after the most gruesome, uncalculated, chaotic, storms.

55

I am in love with me.

56

I don't always have to be G.O.O.D.

G: Graceful

O: Optimistic

O: Open

D: Deliberate

57

Today as I reflect on my life, I will smile realizing I am still here despite what life threw at me.

58

Today's Goal:

Wear the item that you have been putting off for a special occasion. Your life in itself is a special occasion, celebrate it.

59

Today's Goal:

Operate in Love.
In all things,
live, respond
and react from a
place of love.

60

Being Me Is
Enough.

61

My life is worth living.

62

I am worthy of Love.

63

It's ok for me to bend but I will not break;

It's ok for me to cry but I will not be shattered;

It's ok for me to step away for a moment because I WILL come back and continue to stand.

64

Regardless of how long my journey may seem, I will never forget how far I have come.

65

I accept all of me, whether the acceptance of me is a shared space or not.

66

I wasn't created to live a mediocre life: some days you will get the real me and other days you may get my alter ego. Either way it's going to be a hell of a ride.

67

There will be hundreds of thousands of opinions on my life, the funny thing is, the only one I really need is mine.

68

I will remain in a space of expecting good things to happen.

69

I will not get
comfortable in
the discomfort
of conforming.

70

I believe in myself.

71

I can't control
how I am
perceived, but I
can control how I
present myself.

72

I am allowed to walk freely in the skin that I am in.

73

It's ok to be a mess sometimes. The most beautiful pieces of art often come from a place of madness.

74

I do not need
validation from
anyone else to
know who I am.

75

My life is about living not just existing.

76

I don't have to pretend to be anyone else to be seen or heard; My presence and my voice are just enough.

77

Labels are for inanimate objects that can be purchased, not unique human beings that must be cherished.

78

Consider a challenging moment has the potential to be an educating moment.

79

I am thankful for the needed yesses and the very necessary nos.

80

I am grateful for sugar and spice and all the things that are nice.

81

Know when to stand and when to walk away... walking away doesn't scream defeat; more often than not, it screams Victory!

82

There are times that I will have to take my own advice and encourage myself.

83

Consider the respect and acceptance we crave begins with us.

84

One way to love
myself is to
love the
community I am
a part of.

85

When life becomes too much to bear, consider every storm isn't meant just for you. Consider what another can learn from your journey; the power, the resilience, the persistence. Dare to consider the purpose in your pain and the necessity of your journey.

86

I wake-up every day with purpose, on purpose, and for a purpose.

87

I will focus on my gifts and acknowledge my strengths. I may not have someone else's talents but the ones I have aren't too shabby.

88

Time is the universe's way of allowing me the opportunity to share my greatness with the world.

89

Every day I
will wake with
an expectation
that my
contribution to
the world will
make a real
difference.

90

I will love with
intention.

91

Do you ever have a song in your head and as soon as it leaves your mouth, it never quite sounds the same?

Who cares, just keep singing.

92

Today I will recognize that even in the midst of the grey clouds, the sun is still shining.

93

I will not be afraid to ask for help.

94

I deserve the
world and more.

95

Before you think no one else thought of you today, consider the people that wrote this book, wrote it just for you.

96

My happiness is not a detriment to anything or anyone, but, lack thereof would be a detriment to me.

97

Take a moment to look at the bright side; Now consider you are the bright side.

98

If I were wanted any more than I am right now, I would be on a wanted poster. On second thought, maybe I shouldn't be *that* wanted.

99

You can't wake up on the wrong side of the bed if every side is the right side. Keep smiling.

100

There are those that find the solution, and then there those that curse the problem. Which are you?

101

Whenever I feel like I am not needed, I will remember the food in my fridge needs me to eat it, the clothes in my closet needs me to wear it, the items in my online shopping cart need me to buy them, and the people in my life just need me.

102

Take a moment to have your own personal dance party. The best part of having your own dance party is there is no entrance fee and you're the bouncer, bartender, D.J., and the cleaning crew.

103

When in doubt take in extra C.A.R.B.S.

C – confidence/courage/compassion

A – active listening/ambitions/affirmations

R – rewards/respect/relaxation

B – balance/boldness/breaths

S – self-love/self-care/smiles

104

Love is
strength. I
won't be afraid
to love. The
true strength
of a person is
to love in spite
of.

105

I decide what goes
on with my body
and how it is
treated.

106

Every day I will intentionally find a reason to smile.

107

The only reason people don't believe unicorns exist is because I am so good at hiding my identity.

108

How I express myself is my decision to make, not someone else's subject to debate.

109

My body is *my* temple which gives *me* the right to do what *I* want with it.

110

Love worth
fighting for is love
worth keeping.

111

To love with conditions is to love with a closed heart.

112

The storms we endure are never meant to hurt us, they are just the harsh fuel we need in order to bloom during the peak of our season.

113

My words hold power. I will speak words of strength, encouragement, positivity, empowerment, and love (both for self and others).

114

Loving
unconditionally
is like running
through a meadow
without
worrying about
dog poop.

115

All this self-love is making me tired...is it nap time yet?

116

Be human and feel...

beautiful,

powerful,

amazing,

unstoppable,

courageous and

bold.

117

I am a warrior
and my battle
scars prove it.

118

I am important.

What I have to say is important, what I need is important, and what I want is important.

119

This space of
self-doubt,
discouragement
and loneliness
that I am in is
not forever, once
I get past it (*and
I will get past it*)
I will look back
and find that it
was a mere
obstacle in the
triathlon of life.

120

Today's Goal:

Check on a friend.

121

Today's Goal:
Learn to say no; no
to mess, no to
negativity, no to
chaos, no to stuff
that doesn't make
me happy.

122

I have never heard of a love deficit. There is enough love for everyone.

Love is Love

123

Times will get tough, situations will get exhausting and moments will get frustrating but through it all the audacity of my intentional consistency to stay the course will never change.

124

I am not a burden.
Carrying
groceries can be a
burden, paying
never ending
student loans can
be a burden,
sitting in
traffic can also
be considered a
burden but
me...nope, I am not
a burden.

125

Worthless; without value
and importance.

This is everything that I
am NOT, I was born with
value and it grows daily;
the importance of my life
should never be in question;
I wake with a trifecta of
purpose...with purpose, for
a purpose and on purpose.

126

Future Goals:

Just like love is love...

bathroom is bathroom.

127

I am not invisible I am invincible, I am unshakable, capable, and incomparable.

128

Today's Goal:

Ask someone how they are doing and intentionally pause to wait for the answer.

129

Being considered
an "outcast" is
not always a bad
thing, rare gems
always have
their own
"platform" and
every pearl has
its own oyster.

130

Create the kind of circle that makes you want to be a part of it.

131

I am beautiful,
courageous, powerful,
bold, strong, worthy,
deserving, intentional,
positive, intelligent,
funny, unforgettable,
impactful, likeable,
loveable, kind, caring.
I am...

The people that don't live their best lives are the people that can't fathom a unicorn farting glitter.

Instagram: lovebug_mani
E-mail: lwi.andaye@gmail.com

Instagram: Authentic_Author911
E-mail: lwi.ltaitt@gmail.com

BEING ME IS ENOUGH...LGBTQ+

www.ingramcontent.com/pod-product-compliance
Lightning Source LLC
LaVergne TN
LVHW051743080426

835511LV00018B/3208